Wonders of Weather

First English language edition published in 1998 by
New Holland (Publishers) Ltd
London - Cape Town - Sydney - Singapore

24 Nutford Place
London W1H 6DQ
United Kingdom

80 McKenzie Street
Cape Town 8001
South Africa

3/2 Aquatic Drive
Frenchs Forest, NSW 2086
Australia

First published in 1997 in The Netherlands as
Weer Fenomenen by
Holding B. van Dobbenburgh bv, Nieuwkoop,
The Netherlands
Written by: Dr H.F. Vugts & F. Beekman
Translated from the Dutch by: K.M.M. Hudson-Brazenall

ISBN 1-85368-694-8

Editorial direction: D-Books International Publishing
Design: Meijster Design bv
Cover design: M.T. van Dobbenburgh

Reproduction by Unifoto International Pty, Ltd

Technical Production by D-Books International
Publishing/Agora United Graphic Services bv

Printed and bound in Spain by Egedsa, Sabadell

CONTENTS

PHOTO CREDITS

Introduction

Almost everyone has, at some time, lain on their back gazing at the clouds, or watched, from the safety of a house, the lightning strikes of a large thunderstorm. The perpetually changing sky and the continuous exchange of water vapour between earth's surface and the atmosphere provide such fascinating scenes that everyone can admire their beauty. In particular, clouds (and their shapes) have been a source of inspiration and a stimulus for the creation of poetry and paintings (the cloudy skies of Dutch painters).

Although one's first impression is that clouds are chaotic, a close examination of the sky, even by the amateur, reveals that clouds can be classified according tho their shapes. The international cloud classification which is now used worldwide, is based on a simple classification published by the London pharmacist, Luke Howard, in 1803. Howard also achieved fame because the famous poet Johann Wolfgang von Goethe used his classification of clouds in his poems. In this book, Howard's division of clouds into different types is described and illustrated using photographs so that everyone, who makes the effort to look up into the sky, is able to recognise and name them easily. Various cloud types are characteristic for current weather patterns or provide clues to the approaching weather.

As well as the basic types, the many, strikingly beautiful variations in colour and shape of the clouds are shown and how they originate is explained. Other related atmospheric phenomena, like halos (rings around the sun), whirlwinds and lightning strikes are also illustrated in all their glory.

1 Cloud Classification

The classification of clouds used today is still based on the division devised by the London pharmacist, Luke Howard, in his 'Essay on the Modification of Clouds', which was published in 1803. His background in pharmacy meant that he used Latin names for the clouds which made it easier to introduce these names internationally. Their international introduction took place in 1891, during a conference on meteorology in Munich where an extensive classification was proposed and accepted based on Howard's original classification. The three main forms of clouds that Howard had been able to distinguish were: cirrus (wispy), cumulus (woolpack) and stratus (layer mist). In addition, the term nimbus (rain cloud) was also used. The international cloud classification is based on two principles: 1) the form and height and 2) according to how they arise (genesis).

For the names of the ten basic forms, the names as given by Howard are combined. Thus three levels are distinguished: low cloud (less than 2,000 metres), intermediate cloud (2,000–6,000 metres), indicated by the prefix alto, and high cloud (above 6000 metres), indicated by the prefix cirrus or with the derivative cirro. The ten forms are shown below:

Cirrus(Ci): White, thin thread-like plumes or feathers; they are often called 'wind feathers'. They usually have a silky gloss; the sun shines through them almost unaffected and the clouds cast no shadows. In Latin, cirrus means 'curl'.

Cirrostratus (Cs): Evenly distributed cloud with little texture, milky-white in appearance. The sun shines through this as if through frosted glass. These clouds often show some colourful light phenomena, like halos, and are renowned for being harbingers of bad weather.

Cirrocumulus (Cc): Small clouds, often gathered in groups, rows or ripples; they cast no shadows and can sometimes cause wonderful light refraction effects.

Altostratus (As): Dark grey, dull, blanketing layer of cloud. The sun just manages to shine through. It is usually smooth in appearance and shows very few different formations. It can sometimes produce rain.

Altocumulus (Ac): A layer consisting of many balls, or rolls, or it can appear as bands: they are often the cause of attractive colour variations. They are also sometimes known as 'sheep clouds' from their appearance.

Nimbostratus (Ns): Uniformly grey cloud layer with little structure and which often produces persistent rain for hours at a time. The cloud layer is thick enough to hide the sun. It is the classic bad weather cloud.

Stratus(St): A structureless grey cloud layer, close to the ground, sometimes originating as lifting fog. Rain almost never falls from this type of cloud, at most it produces drizzle. Fog also falls into this cloud category.

Stratocumulus (Sc): The cloud elements are often found in banks or in a layer of alternate lighter and darker areas.

Cumulus (Cu): individual cloud that develops particularly in a vertical direction several hours after sunrise. Sometimes they lie in rows. They are usually smooth on the underside and irregular on top. Towards evening, cumulus clouds generally just disperse.

Cumulonimbus (Cb): This is clearly a storm cloud, well developed vertically, often with an anvil top. They are often awe-inspiring and manifest the immense natural power of the ascending air currents.

Photographing clouds is in itself a specialist subject. Simply pointing the camera upwards generally does not produce the best images. By including part of the landscape in the photograph, the dramatic nature of the cloud formation is highlighted. The mirror effect and the dark/light contrast of the photograph to the right, give the 'sheep clouds' a totally different dimension.

2 How Clouds Predict the Weather

Some types of clouds, or the sequence of certain types of clouds, can indicate a change in the weather or the approach of a warm or cold front that will be accompanied by rain. Using the changes in the clouds, the interested amateur can estimate how quickly the precipitation will reach him and can, therefore, make his own weather forecast. First, we will explain the processes that occur in the atmosphere so that we are better able to understand what we are observing.

The weather is, to a great extent, determined by the movement of high and low pressure areas; the latter are also called 'depressions'. The air masses set in motion by these areas of high and low pressure, each with their own different characteristics like dry and warm or damp and cold, often remain distinct from each other. The boundary between two different sorts of air is called the 'frontal zone'. This zone is not flat but lies at a slight slope. The imaginary line between the frontal zone and the earth's surface is called the 'front'. In the vicinity of depressions these fronts form active weather areas and are characteristic of changes in the weather. We talk of a warm or cold front depending on whether warm or cold air is moving towards us. The

Example of a cloud formation, cirrus fibratus, also known as 'wind feathers'.

In cirrostratus a halo, or at least part of one, can usually be seen; this small ring lies at 22° from the sun in the cirrostratus nebulosus clouds.

With the approach of a warm front, the cirrostratus gradually expands to lower levels where it forms altostratus, a combination of the two cloud types.

stereotypical sequence of events witnessed when a warm front passes, is as follows (see figure below). The warm air (which is lighter) slides up over the cold air (which is heavier) and cirrus and cirrostratus clouds form at high altitude. The upwards motion is accompanied by strong, vertical air movements along the frontal zone that stimulate the increase in cloud. The cloud cover gradually becomes thicker and produces altostratus and nimbostratus clouds that give rain or snow.

An observer watching the approach of a warm front from a great distance, will first see high cirrus clouds appear above the horizon. These are loose wisps, thread-like in structure and usually with curls (cirrus uncinus). The closer the front approaches to the observer, the thicker the cirrus becomes, and this creates a more uniform layer through which the sun or moon shines as if through opaque glass and casts shadows. This type of cloud is called cirrostratus. Often a ring appears around the sun, a 'halo', a word that stems from the Greek word *halos*, meaning 'ring' or 'bow'. The rings around the sun or moon have a radius of 22° or 46°. They occur through the refraction and diffraction of either sunlight or moonlight in the ice crystals present in the clouds. These crystals all have the same form and size and are also all oriented in the same direction. The appearance of 'mock suns' horizontally to the left or right can also be observed at times. The next stage is that the cirrostratus cloud cover thickens, blocking out more of the sun, whilst the cloud base lowers continually and eventually takes on the altostratus form.

The cloud cover is thick enough to produce much precipitation (nimbostratus).

◁*The sun can no longer be seen (altostratus opacus).*

Finally, the observer will see nimbostratus clouds overhead. It will rain at the same intensity for many hours from the thick cirrostratus-altostratus-nimbostratus package before the true front passes at ground level. In the meantime, the visibility will generally have been considerably reduced, and will remain so for some time after the passage of the front. As the front passes the wind will then veer (shift in a clockwise direction, that is from south-west to west) and the temperature will rise. A couple of hours after the passage of the front at ground level, the rain stops. The sight of cirrus clouds that continue to thicken, together with accompanying optical phenomena, gives about 70% certainty of rain within a day. The saying: 'A ring around the sun or moon, means that rain will come real soon', fits this prediction (see Weather Proverbs p.66).

How clouds occur

Water vapour is a necessary component for the creation of clouds, and this occurs in varying quantities in the atmosphere: above the sea there is plenty of water vapour and above deserts very little. As we rise through the atmosphere the quantity of water vapour steadily reduces, so that above 20 kilometres high, there is only a minute amount of water vapour. For any specific temperature there is a definite limit to the quantity of moisture that can be held by the air. This limit is known as the 'saturation point', but the higher the temperature, the more water vapour the air can contain. Usually the air will contain less than the maximum amount of water vapour, and a frequently used measure of this is the relative humidity: the relationship between the existing amount of water vapour

Air molecules become warmer above land than above water in the daytime. They therefore rise to greater altitudes, causing condensation and cloud formation to take place only above land.

14

and the maximum amount of water vapour, expressed as a percentage. Clouds occur if the relative humidity is 100% or higher. The water vapour then condenses forming droplets or, if the temperature is below 0°C, ice crystals. There are two ways that the relative humidity can reach 100%. The first way is when water vapour is added to the air and the second way, that happens most frequently in nature, is through cooling the air. When air rises, it cools, which happens when it is forced to rise over mountain ridges, in frontal zones and in depressions. Water vapour does not condense just like that, for it requires some kind of particle either to condense onto or to sublimate. These are the so-called 'condensation' or 'freezing nuclei'. Condensation nuclei occur in great numbers: from a few thousand per cubic centimetre above clean regions to a few million per cubic centimetre above towns and industrial regions. They may have natural origins: the sea, (dispersed salt crystals), bush fires (carbon particles) and volcanic eruptions (dust particles); and they may also be produced by human activities: industry and traffic. Freezing nuclei occur less often: on

Clear freezing air and bare trees forma picturesque combination in this wide-angle shot.

In the morning, when the earth's surface is warmed by the sun, mist disperses and stratus or cumulus fractus forms temporarily at a higher altitude.

Sheep clouds have a ribbed appearance, caused by wave movements in the atmosphere. For this reason, they are called altocumulus undulatus.

Different types of cloud can be present at the same time, but underneath each other. Underneath we see cumulus mediocris; above, the thread-like wisps of cirrus uncinus.

The rear of the cold front, as it moves away, remains visible as a wall of cumulus congestus and cumulonimbus. The grey stripes of cloud belong to the cloud type altocumulus lenticularis.

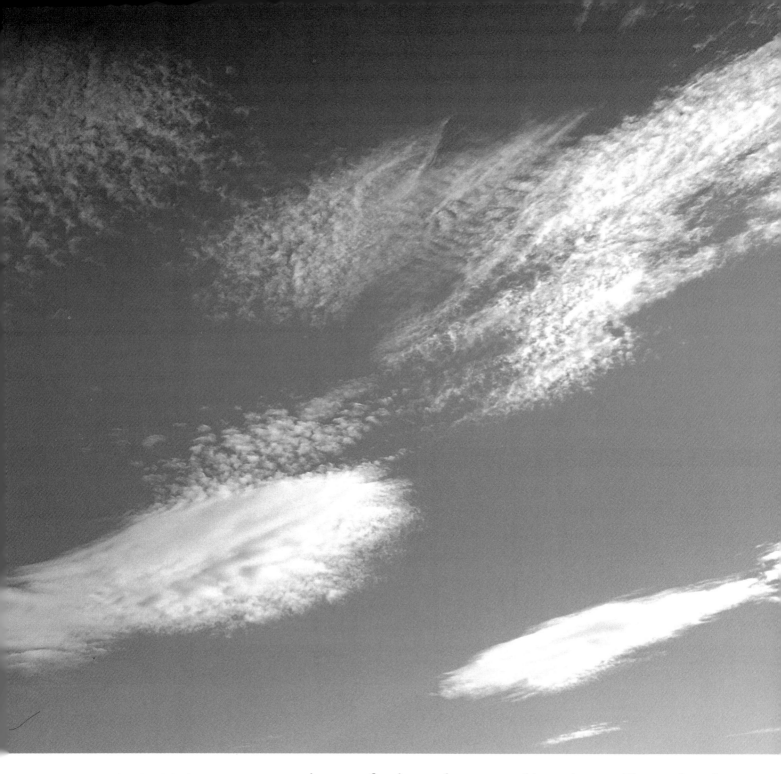

These lens-shaped clouds (altocumulus lenticularis) are subject to evaporation. The atmosphere at intermediate altitude is dry: good weather is on the way.

▷Two examples of 'heavy skies': the sun is still just shining in the foreground and on the dark underside of the cumulonimbi.

average there are a few thousand per 1,000 cubic centimetres. They need to take the form of a crystal to be able to function as a freezing nucleus. The droplets and ice crystals formed through condensation are called cloud elements and are very tiny, being no greater than 0.01 to 0.1 millimetre in diameter. They have to grow considerably, before raindrops develop. Two processes are responsible for this: the 'coalescence process' and the 'Wegener-Bergeron-Findeisen process'. In the coalescence process, the droplets bump into each other and join up, forming a few large droplets, which then fall faster than the smaller droplets. As they fall, they bump into the smaller droplets and are able to continue growing in this way until they achieve the size of a precipitation element, when they are large enough to reach the earth's surface without evaporating on the way. The drop size is a maximum of 1 millimetre. The Wegener-Bergeron-Findeisen process occurs particularly in cold, mixed clouds in which supercooled water droplets and ice crystals exist alongside each other. In this situation the ice crystals grow at the expense of the droplets. They may finally reach the earth's surface as drops with a diameter of 1 to 10 millimetres, or as large snow flakes.

18

3 Thunder and Lightning

▷A discharge between earth and cloud. The temperature in the tract where the 'spark' jumps is, for about 40 microseconds, raised to some 25,000℃.

Precipitation that can be observed reaching the ground under a far-distant shower cloud is known as (Cumulonimbus) praecipitatio.

In a rain cloud, differences in electrical charge can be built up as a result of strong up-and-down drafts. The difference in charge is boosted by the freezing of supercooled water droplets, which occurs optimally at a temperature of -12℃. The lightest particles, which are positively charged, are carried to the top of the cloud, whilst the heavier, negative particles can be found at the base of the cloud. The result of this is that the earth's surface below the cloud becomes positively charged. If the difference in potential between the ground and the cloud is large enough (about two million volts) then a discharge will occur: a short sharp electrical surge follows. Usually there is first a pre-discharge, which we often cannot see, which is then followed by the main discharge in the direction from the earth to the cloud. The surge of electricity, which can be several tens of thousands of amperes, heats the air to about 25,000℃ causing it to expand rapidly; this is heard by us as a bang. Discharges can also occur between clouds; then we see horizontal lightning.

This photograph shows several lightning disharges. It was taken using a longer shutter time during the exposure.

Horizontal discharges within the cloud.

It is possible for several discharges to take place one after the other in the same tract. This causes the flash to flicker.

4 Whirlwinds, Tornadoes, Dust and Sand Storms

In very unstable weather, whirlwinds or tornadoes can occur in combination with heavy showers. Other conditions that contribute to their occurrence are the wind speed, which must rapidly increase with height and the wind direction, which must also change considerably with an increase in height. These factors allow dry, cold air to be drawn in at an intermediate height. As a result of mixing with damp air that has been violently drawn up from the earth's surface, the rising air gains even more speed and acquires a rotating motion. Once the rotating motion has begun properly, then the air pressure in the innermost section starts to drop, allowing the central column to extend downwards. This is what becomes easily visible once it falls below the cloud level, because of the water vapour in its core. The column narrows towards the bottom to form a funnel that, once it touches the ground, draws up dust and all kinds of small objects. Above the surface of water, such funnels draw up water, thereby creating water spouts. If the funnel is several metres across, then we talk of a whirlwind; the funnels of tornadoes are larger and have a diameter of several hundreds of metres. They can cause an enormous amount of damage in a very short time. Water spouts occur when a cold air mass passes over the surface of warm water. They are, for this reason, much more common in the late summer and autumn, above coastal waters and large lakes.

Even if the funnel of a whirlwind, a water spout or a dust devil is not or only partially visible, the corkscrewing action of the air can still be present at ground level; they do not always betray their presence with a funnel...

Last but not least we have 'dust devils'. These occur, in particular, above steppes, deserts, sandy areas and bare, agricultural land. This phenomenon only occurs if the air mass is unstable and it is at least 40 °C on the ground. The rapidly rising air, which turns around a core as in a whirlwind, can rise to anything between several tens to hundreds of metres in height. Since the air in the funnel cannot be quickly removed, as in a tornado, condensation heat is not released and the dust devil collapses within

In Texas (USA) and the surrounding states in particular, there are many tornadoes. The majority occur in the spring, when warm, moist air from the Gulf of Mexico meets cold, dry air from the Rocky Mountains.

◁This cumulonimbus tuba cloud spawned a whirlwind on 28 August 1993 just to the north of Ostend (Belgium), which was observed from a sport plane at a distance of 200 metres. The funnel did not actually reach the ground.

The funnel of a tornado consists of condensed water vapour and dust and objects sucked up into it. The width is generally less than 150 metres, but can, in extreme situations, be as wide as several kilometres.

25

In the few minutes that a tornado takes to race through an area, enormous devastation can occur. In addition to human suffering, the material damage that one tornado can cause often amounts to millions of dollars.

a few minutes. The dust or sand they suck up makes them highly visible.

In the USA there are, on average, between 500 and 600 tornadoes annually. Fujita and Pearson developed a table to allow comparisons to be made between the strengths of different tornadoes. They distinguished six different classes: F (Force) 0 to F5.

Scale Category	Wind speed(km/h)		Damage
F0	Weak	0–116	Slight
F1	Weak	117–180	Moderate
F2	Powerful	181–253	Considerable
F3	Powerful	254–332	Enormous
F4	Violent	333–418	Immense
F5	Violent	419–496	Unprecedented

One of the most deadly tornadoes in the USA was the Tri-State Tornado. On 18

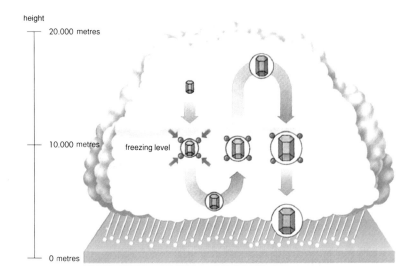

26

March 1925 this tornado killed almost 700 people on its rampage through Missouri, Illinois and Indiana. The hail that falls in the winter season in temperate regions is, in most cases, 'pearl hail'. The largest hailstones, however, fall in the summer months, when heavier (thunder) showers develop above the land in the course of the day as a result of the increased instability of the atmosphere. In particular, hail showers cause great problems for the agricultural sector. In the USA, the Denver region is a regular setting for very heavy hailstone showers. On 11 July 1990 a shower there caused $600 million dollars' worth of damage.

The diameter of hailstones in coastal regions in temperate latitudes is generally between 5 and 50 millimetres. In the USA, hailstones the size of baseballs hit the ground occasionally.

Tropical cyclones

Tropical cyclones are depressions with an average diameter of 500 kilometres, that arise above warm oceanic water between 10° and 20° north and south of the equator. Scientific research has shown that the temperature of the sea water has to be at least 26.5°C for the creation of a tropical cyclone to form. This means that they occur in the northern hemisphere, especially from the end of August through September and October, and in the southern hemisphere, from the end of February, through March and April. The tropical cyclone draws its energy, with wind speeds often in excess of 100 kilometres per hour, from the condensation heat that is released when clouds form within the area of low pressure. Their life cycle is approximately one week since they are rapidly extinguished when they come on land (due to a lack of moisture) or meet colder water. They are easy to recognise on satellite pictures, which show the clouds grouped in a spiral around the cloud-free centre of the cyclone, called the 'eye'.

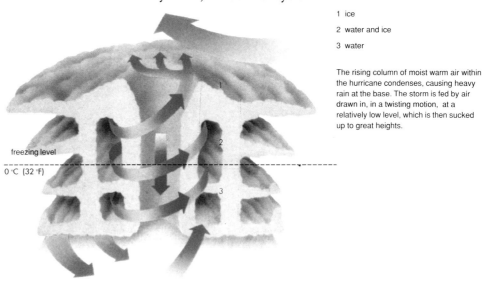

1 ice

2 water and ice

3 water

The rising column of moist warm air within the hurricane condenses, causing heavy rain at the base. The storm is fed by air drawn in, in a twisting motion, at a relatively low level, which is then sucked up to great heights.

If a tropical storm has developed into a tropical cyclone then the 'eye' can usually be observed on various satellite images. The direction of movement of the cyclone can then be followed and predicted more accurately.

With high wind speeds, waves can be thrown metres high into the air.

When a river bursts its banks, the speed of the flow reduces.

A peripheral effect of tropical cyclones is the huge waves that result from both the drop in pressure in the centre of the cyclone and water pushed up by the wind. These waves are responsible for a great deal of damage along coasts and in harbours.

Tropical cyclones frequently occur in the Caribbean region where they are called hurricanes. Along the east coast of China they are called typhoons and on the north coast of Australia they go by the name of 'willy-willies'. To distinguish one cyclone from another, they are alternately given the names of boys or girls in alphabetical order, starting each year with the letter A.

5 Mist

Amongst amateur meteorologists, mist and fog have always been considered wonderful sources of accurate predictions about the weather to come. To understand this, we must first look in depth at the way mist or fog arises. Whenever cold air lies above relatively warm ground, then the relative humidity of the air mass can reach 100% through the following mechanism. Water vapour saturates the air close to the warm ground, which then mixes with the colder air so that the humidity in the mixed air mass increases and over-saturation occurs. The result is condensation that is visible to us as mist, which, in everyday life, we can easily observe forming along ditches in fields after sunset. The land cools faster than the water in the ditches and the air above the land also becomes colder than the air above the ditches. The result is that this cold air, being heavier than warm air, sinks into the ditches which lie lower, forcing the displacement of the warm air above the ditches. Through the mixing of the cold air with this warmer air, 'ditch fog', as it is called, forms. A similar phenomenon occurs to the east of the Labrador coastline, where the cold air carried on the north wind from Canada and Greenland, comes into contact with one of the offshoots of the (warm) Gulf Stream. Through mixing of both air types, over-saturation occurs and fog forms that carries the poetic name of 'Arctic smoke'. This fog layer can be several tens of metres thick and lingers for a long time.

At night, cold air from the sides displaces the relatively warm air above the lake. Close to the warmer water surface, the air rises and immediately condenses. This causes mist to form above the water.

Apart from raising the relative humidity by adding water vapour, mist can also form through the cooling of the air. When the sky is cloudless at night and there is practically no wind, the earth cools through radiation whereby the temperature of the air above the earth's surface falls rapidly. The result of this fall in temperature is that the relative humidity of the air increases, causing the air to become saturated. Condensation then takes place and a type of fog arises that is called 'radiation fog'. If there is no wind, then the fog layer is only a few metres thick and may also be known as ground fog. In the summer this fog rapidly dissipates in the early morning, in contrast to colder times of the year when it can be more persistent.

The low position of the sun soon after sunrise casts long shadows behind the trees in the dispersing mist. Through the intense scattering of the light, the shadows and the illuminated areas are merged into a diffuse whole.

Fog and mist may also occur when very humid warm air passes over a cold surface. If the air is sufficiently cooled, then the relative humidity rises to its maximum value and condensation then forms. The fog thus formed is called 'advective fog', which means it is carried horizontally. This kind of fog occurs particularly in coastal regions in the autumn and winter, when a warm air mass passes over a cold body of water.

In meteorology, the term 'mist' or 'thin fog' is used when visibility drops below 1,000 metres. In general, problems only arise for road traffic once the visibility falls below 200 metres (dense fog) with more severe consequences once visibility drops to less than 50 metres (very dense fog). Notably, the first dense fog or banks of fog in the autumn cause real trouble for the traffic on the roads. Dense fog is still one of the most important causes of delays to the air traffic industry. If dense fog is forecast for an aircraft's destination, then more fuel has to be loaded to allow the plane to divert to an alternative airport.

△▷Slowly dispersing mist, photographed at two different points in time, early and late in the afternoon. The change in colour is clear to see.

If the mist or stratus is thin, or if it is only very hazy, then the sun or moon will shine through as if through frosted glass (stratus translucidus).

The mist has formed only in the river valley, the coldest and dampest place, and remains there for a considerable time. Above, under an inversion (warmer air layer) lies a layer of dispersing stratocumulus.

6 Snow and Ice

The volume of fresh water that is present on earth in the form of ice is approximately 32 million cubic kilometres.

This quantity of ice covers almost 16 million square kilometres of the earth's surface, which is slightly more than 3% of the total surface area of the earth and about 11% of the continental land mass. During the last ice age about a quarter of the continents were covered with ice, but of the ice now present, about 90% of it can be found in Antarctica; the remainder can be found in Greenland and on the smaller ice caps and glaciers. If all the ice were to melt, then sea level would rise by about 70 metres. Nearly all of the ice now present fell as snow at a temperature of 0°C or lower. In temperate zones, where precipitation can only fall as snow in the winter, and any snow cover disappears after a while, then snow falls can produce wonderful scenes, but they are also capable of causing huge inconvenience to both man and animals. In a snowstorm, for example, the wind can drive the snow into banks as high as houses, thus making roads impassable. Snowploughs have

The drifting snow gathers in sheltered spots behind houses or hedges. Huge snowdrifts can build up, isolating the inhabitants.

Falling snow has clumped together to form thick snowflakes; the temperature is higher than -5°C. With hard frost the flakes are smaller and are known as 'powder snow'.

When supercooled rain falls on a surface, it freezes immediately. The same is true of rain that is not supercooled but falls on frozen ground or other frozen objects. In both cases this is called 'glaze ice' or 'freezing rain'.

The hoar frost slowly grows through the continuing condensation of water vapour, at a temperature below freezing, producing needles of ice.

to be brought in to clear the roads, and salt and grit have to be spread, entailing considerable expense. In the mountains, the snow can pile up in sheltered areas to form snowdrifts, whilst overhanging snow masses are then able to accumulate, which, should they happen to break off, can cause avalanches...

Ice deposits

Frost occurs through the sublimation of water vapour on surfaces at temperatures below 1°C. Frost consists of a very thin layer of ice crystals that sometimes produces attractive fan-shaped structures. 'Hoar frost' arises when supercooled fog bumps into immovable objects such as trees. Hoar frost is white and looks 'hairy'.

Freezing rain occurs when supercooled raindrops freeze. This situation occurs particularly when a thaw sets in after a frost period. Since the ground is frozen (sometimes to quite a depth), the air temperature is also below freezing for several tens of metres above the ground. In the layer of warm, thawing air above this, the raindrops that fall from the clouds are above 0°C, but become supercooled just above the ground. They only freeze once they have hit the ground, roofs, twigs or other objects, changing into transparent ice. A tough glass-like layer of ice is created. If this happens on the road surface then it can lead to very dangerous situations; if freezing rain lands on trees then this can produce fairytale-like scenes.

◁Super-cooled mist droplets can freeze onto objects. Together with freezing rain, this kind of hoar frost can be problematic for electricity and telephone cables because of the weight on the cables.

In regions where snow is plentiful, the sides of the road are often marked with poles so that the snowploughs can find the road when it is snowed under.

7 Cloud Formations

Wave form clouds

Whenever two substances with a different density and a different speed move past each other, a wave will arise on the interface. This can, for example, be easily seen when water has passed over sand (ripples) or wind over a water surface (waves). In the atmosphere, two different air masses can move over each other and when the temperature difference is great enough, then there will also be sufficient difference in density. Wave movement occurs along the interface, which means that we see upward and downward air movements, one after the other. In the upward air

The dark streaks of cloud are also known as cumulus fractus.

This cloud is the type altocumulus lenticularis. This cloud form often remains stationary for hours and is sometimes mistaken for a flying saucer. Nausori Highlands, Fiji, 1990.

This altocumulus lenticularis which has occured on the leeside of a mountain ridge, belongs to the so-called 'orographical clouds' (determined by relief). Differences in humidity in air layers lying above each other, often result in a layered appearance. Tiede, Tenerife, 1995.

This stratus-like lenticularis form can be tens of kilometres long. It is indicative of strong winds at greater altitude, which become turbulent when flowing over a mountain ridge. It occurs in clear air. Sierra Nevada, USA, 1993.

This cloud layer at medium height
(between 2.5 and 6 km high)
consists of supercooled water
droplets. The name given by
Howard to this cloud type is
'altoculumus stratiformus'.

movements condensation then occurs and undulatus clouds develop. They occur particularly as altocumulus undulatus and stratocumulus undulatus. The banks of cloud lie at right angles to the air flow. When an air flow passes a mountain or hill ridge, then a wave movement can form on the lee side. In the upward sections, clouds of the altocumulus lenticularis type (lens-shaped) may form.

Mamma clouds

The 'mamma cloud' formation occurs particularly at the base, the thicker and lower part, of a cumulonimbus cloud. They are often to be found at the leading edge, or even ahead, of the shower. These purse-shaped bulges arise because the precipitation elements that have formed, for example raindrops, hailstones or snowflakes, evaporate before they manage to reach the ground: the air under the leading edge of the cloud is still too warm to allow precipitation. The descending cold air stream creates counter-flows of air at the leading edge so that lighter and darker spots are visible on the underside of the cloud formation. The lighter and darker spots represent the rising and falling air movements and can be observed best when the sun is low.

Cirrus uncinus ('comma clouds').

The streaks of falling rain (virga) from a shower can be seen in the middle of the photograph. On the underside a bank of cloud consisting of cumulus mediocris can be seen.

Fall streaks

Streaks of falling rain can be observed whenever rain or snow falls from clouds that are at a high altitude. Through evaporation in the course of their fall, the drops become steadily smaller or disappear altogether. We are able to observe a veil of precipitation with increasingly thinner, downwards pointing tips. If the tip of the veil fails to reach the ground then the phenomenon is known as 'virga'. Sometimes we see at some distance that the rain streaks do actually reach the ground, a phenomenon called 'praecipitatio'.

Rolling cloud formation

Sometimes a 'rolling cloud' formation is found on the leading edge of a rain cloud. They occur on the interface between the descending, cold air and the warm, rising air of the rain cloud. Whirlwinds with a horizontal axis occur on this interface, which greatly stimulate the mixing of the warm and cold air masses to form condensation of water vapour and a cloud with a cylindrical form occurs.

The earth viewed from space at a height of 36,000 kilometres. This image was taken in infra-red by the geostationary satellite 'METEOSAT'. Everything that is white is cold, and depicts high cloud formations. The thick white tufts of cloud above Africa are clusters of thunderstorms.

Weather satellites

The advent of weather satellites in 1960 brought better insights into the spatial distribution of clouds and the structure of cloud systems. The cell structure and ranking of banks of cumulus clouds can be distinguished easily on satellite pictures. In particular, tropical cyclones and the curled shape of depressions are clearly recognisable, which provides significant help in drawing up a weather forecast.

The two most important satellites for meteorologists are the NOAA satellite and METEOSAT. NOAA rotates at approximately 800 kilometres high around the earth from pole to pole. The advantage of this rotation is that the satellite looks at the earth mostly straight down and, given its low altitude, can make beautiful, detailed images. However, it is only overhead a couple of times a day. The METEOSAT satellite lies in a geostationary orbit some 36,000 kilometres above the equator, and is therefore always in the same place. Every half hour, images of a large area (Africa and Europe) are sent back to earth. One disadvantage of this satellite is that, apart

◁The last remnants of a rain cloud. From the thread-like structure of the rain streaks it can be seen that the precipitation is solid: it is snowing.

45

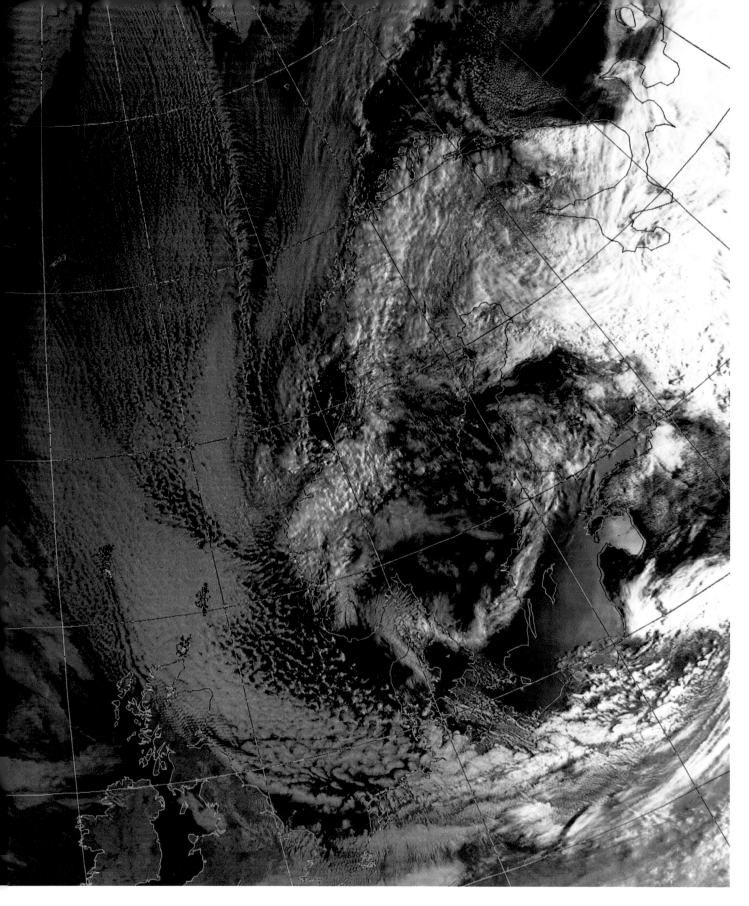

North-west Europe and
Scandinavia, seen from the NOAA
satellite orbiting pole to pole at a
height of c. 850 kilometres. This

image, from 16 April 1991, was
taken in visible light as can be seen
from the sun glint above the Baltic
Sea. On this photo a wave pattern

of clouds can be seen, caused by the
Norwegian island of Jan Mayen,
and a pattern with cloud ripples
created by the Scottish Highlands.

The banks of clouds, like those
behind Jan Mayen Island, consist
of cumulus clouds which can also be
called string clouds.

from the region of the equator, it looks down obliquely, thus producing a slightly
distorted image. These images are nearly always entirely corrected before they reach
the users. In addition to the transmission of visible images of the kind we are
familiar with from television weather reports, the satellites also take measurements,
one of which is the infra-red radiation of water vapour.

An infra-red image of a section of the Atlantic Ocean, made by the NOAA satellite on 15 December 1986. A mega-depression with a core pressure of about 920 millibars to the south west of Iceland caused heavy showers in a trough, lying from just to the west of Ireland to Iceland. Above Greenland, much cirrus, in particular, has gathered.

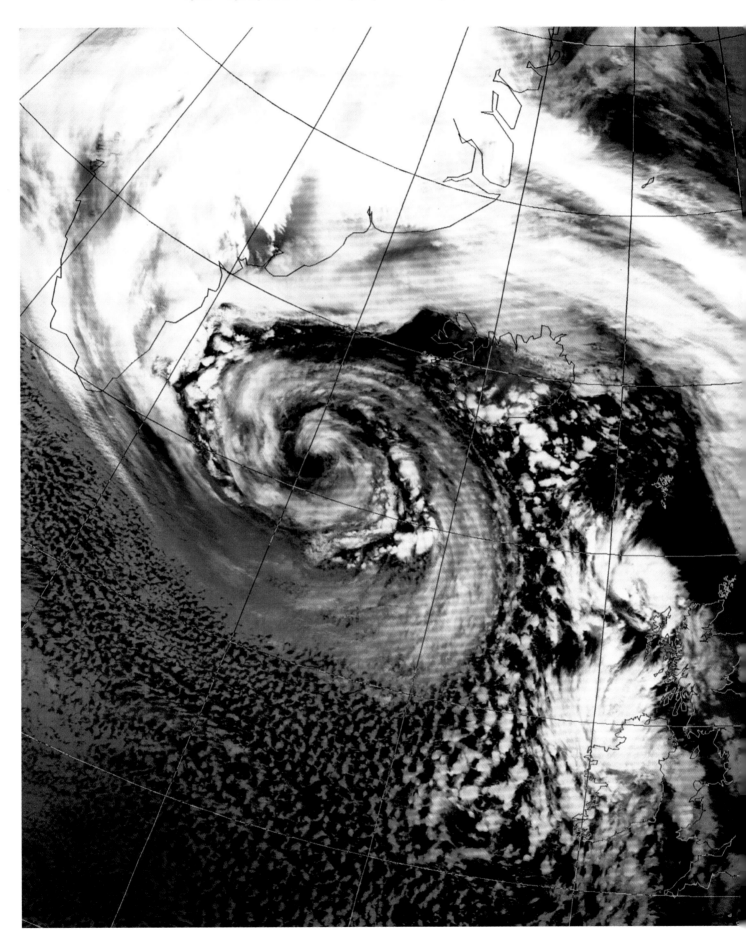

This image, taken in visible light by NOAA satellite 11 on 28 February 1989, shows Iceland on the right hand side and Greenland at the top. Magnificent swirls behind Iceland are caused by the 1446 metre-high Snaeffellsjokull. Just to the north of Iceland pack ice can be seen. Snow is lying in many places on both Iceland and Greenland.

Cloud patterns behind obstacles

When cold air streams southwards in the spring from Greenland over the relatively warm sea water, then rows of clouds may form (these are sometimes called 'string clouds') that lie parallel to the direction of the wind. If this cold air then meets an obstacle, such as Jan Mayen Island or the Faeroes Islands, then 'Von Karman' vortices of cloud can form behind these obstacles. In the photograph above, they can be seen alternately lying to the east and west of Jan Mayen Island, where we can observe two equidistant swirls.

48

8 Optical Phenomena

Haloes

A halo is a ring of light around the sun or the moon, caused by the refraction of the sunlight in ice crystals present high in the atmosphere. Halo phenomena only appear when the cloud cover is uniform and thin enough, and is of the form cirrostratus. The ice crystals have to be the same shape and size, whilst they also have to be aligned in approximately the same direction. The small halo around the sun occurs quite frequently. The angle to the sun is then 22°. The circle can simply be a clear band but different colours can also be observed at times. The inside of the ring is usually pale red. The large ring, where the angle to the sun is 46°, does not occur as frequently. In general it is less clear but more splendidly coloured. Often a

49

◁▷Halo.

column can be seen: a light streak above or below the sun; tangential bows above or below the sun may also be observed. The latter lie with the curved side turned towards the sun. Finally, we should also mention 'mock suns' or 'parhelions': these are often brightly coloured light spots to the left and right of the sun.

A column rises straight up from the setting sun.

Nacreous clouds

The phenomenon of 'nacreous' (or 'mother-of-pearl') clouds occurs in intermediate and high altitude clouds, in particular altocumulus. The clouds often demonstrate a brilliant mother-of-pearl gloss. The colours green, purplish-red or blue are the clearest at a few degrees from the sun. This may be hidden from the naked eye by a (thicker) cloud, mountain top or a man-made object (building). The iridescence is an interference phenomenon that occurs by means of the refraction and reflection of the sunlight in ice crystals.

Light effects in cirrus uncinus.

Mother-of-pearl colours in cirrus vertebratus.

Rainbows and mist bows

A rainbow in the morning,
Is the shepherd's warning.
A rainbow at night,
Is the shepherd's delight.

Rainbows can be seen when the sun is low and the weather is showery. To
see one, the observer must stand with his back to the sun whilst it
illuminates a curtain of rain. The white sunlight that passes through the
raindrops, is split into its spectral colours through refraction and simple
reflection on the inside of the drop. Maximum intensity occurs if the beams

*A double rainbow. Light that does
not contribute to the colours of the
rainbow itself, causes an increase in
the light intensity on the inside of
the main rainbow and on the
outside of the subsidiary rainbow.*

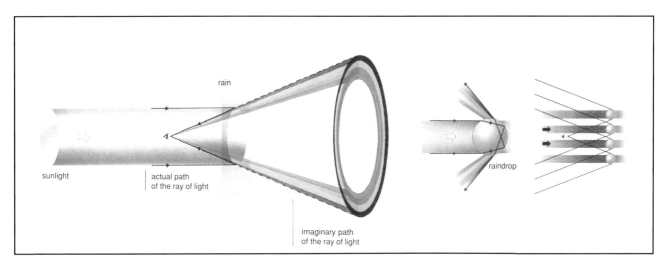

53

On the inside of a rainbow, particularly towards the top, several bows can often be seen. This is caused by light interference in the droplets. The bows are also known as 'supernumery bows'.

The clear inner and outer side of the rainbow shows up well. And the cows? They continue to graze, oblivious to the wonders of nature.

of light that have been coloured, form an angle of 40° with the light bundle entering the drop. This also explains why in the summer, we only see rainbows in the early morning and evening, whilst in the winter, rainbows can be observed throughout the day. Given that the red light is reflected at a greater angle than the violet light, on the outside the rainbow is coloured red whilst violet adorns the inside. If there is a double reflection in the drops, then we can see a subsidiary rainbow at an angle of about 52° that is not nearly so distinct, with reversed colours: red on the inside and violet on the outside. On the inside of the main rainbow, small, more weakly coloured secondary rainbows can often be observed.

When sunlight falls on mist droplets a 'mist bow' can occur. They are, however, much less spectacular because they are colourless or nearly colourless.

In the early morning, the light of the newly risen sun refracts in the very fine droplets of fog, mist or dew. This can sometimes cause an almost colourless 'mist' or 'dew bow' to appear.

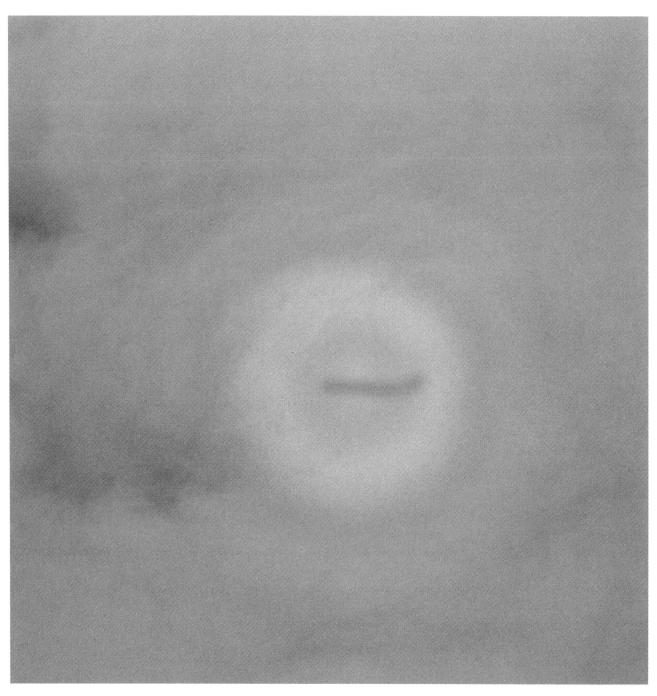

With the sun on the opposite side of the plane, a 'glory' can very often be seen from the plane on the cloud cover below. The observer is himself the centre point of the coloured ring.
▷ 'Sainted light' around the photographer's head.

Glory, sainted light and aeroplane contrails

If an aeroplane is illuminated by the sun and its shadow is cast on the clouds, then coloured rings can be seen around that shadow. This phenomenon is called 'glory'. When the sun is low, in the morning and evening and then particularly on (damp) grass, a pale whitish ring can be observed around the long shadow of a person, the so-called 'sainted light'.

In certain circumstances white trails can be seen behind high flying aeroplanes. These are artificially created clouds formed by the exhaust gases of the aeroplanes. The exhaust gases contain water vapour and condensation nuclei, which, at a distance from the aeroplane, cool off and allow condensation to form, thus producing clouds. This is why such clouds are called 'contrails', derived from the words 'condensation' and 'trails'. After a while they break up, having mixed with the dry air around them. However, if the air is really cold, that is lower than -55℃, then the trails remain very compact and are slow to disperse.

The aurora borealis (northern lights)

The aurora borealis (northern lights), also called the 'polar lights', is a light phenomenon that is particularly easy to observe in the area around the Northern Arctic Circle. The phenomenon can also be seen close to the South Pole where it is called the aurora australis (southern lights). The word 'aurora' is derived from the name of the Roman goddess of the dawn. The further one travels away from the North Pole the less the chance of seeing them. The polar lights are to be seen high up in the atmosphere, that is at a height of between 100 and 1,000 kilometres. However, they usually display their beauty at a height of between 75 and 150 kilometres. The phenomenon is caused by an increase in the sun's activity, whereby fast (approximately 1,600 kilometres per second) electrically charged particles enter the

A bow with vague streaks. The aurora borealis (in the southern hemisphere known as aurora australis or southern lights) can appear in various guises.

atmosphere and raise the energy levels of the atoms and ions in the upper layers of the atmosphere. When they return to their original energy levels then polar light is transmitted. This manifests itself as a waving curtain of light or light bundles with beautiful colours in the northern and southern skies. The occurrence of polar lights coincides with the sunspot maximum, when the sun shows its greatest activity, also giving this phenomenon an eleven year cycle.

An aurora borealis in the form of a 'curtain' can be observed between the moon and stars.

Northern lights in the form of stripes or beams. The beams lie in line with the earth's magnetic field.

△ A 'curtain' of light. Usually the northern lights are red or green in colour as a result of oxygen atoms; violet, caused by nitrogen atoms, is rarer.

▷'Beams' joining in the upper left corner of the photograph to form the 'corona'.

▷△▷▽Beams that join up in the 'corona', above left in the photograph.

9 Colours in the Atmosphere

Red skies at night,
Shepherd's delight.
Red skies in the morning,
Shepherd's warning.

For those who regularly look at the sky, it is common knowledge that not only blues and greys colour the skies but that, besides the stereotypical yellow, orange-red sunset and sunrise, almost all colours can be seen. This is because white sunlight, in principle, contains all colours, the so-called sun spectrum. Depending on the atmospheric conditions, these colours will be separated, resulting in colourful scenes that are a source of inspiration for painters, poets and composers.

When a lot of dust is in the atmosphere, especially after a volcanic eruption, the sky colours to a deep red after sunset. Here it is twilight and the full spectrum of colours can be seen.

The blue of the sky is the result of diffusion of the white light in its journey through the atmosphere. This diffusion by air molecules, such as nitrogen and oxygen, does not occur equally for the different spectral colours; the smaller the wave length of the light, the greater the diffusion. This means, for instance that the blue light is much more strongly diffused than the red light. Consequently, blue light, and not very much light of any other colour, shines on our eyes from all directions except from the direction of the sun. The entire impression of the sky is therefore blue. In Western Europe the purest blue can be seen in the late winter and early spring, especially when air from northerly climes flows over the region. This air is almost entirely free of pollution and contains little water vapour so that diffusion only occurs on air molecules.

In many circumstances, however, the air contains particles that are larger than the air molecules. The diffusion of the various colours is then more uniform, making the blue of the sky paler. This can be seen particularly when the sun is low in the vicinity of large cities where the atmosphere is turbid. Even larger particles in the atmosphere diffuse the light equally so that we are left with a white impression, as if the sun was shining through a cloud. The most fascinating colour spectacle can be experienced from about one hour before, to one hour after sunset or sunrise. Due to the sun's low position, the light has to travel further through the lowest layer of the atmosphere. Here, it bumps into more dust or other particles and therefore

Once the sun has disappeared beyond the horizon it does not become dark immediately. Twilight lasts about 15 to 30 minutes.

Atmospheric and colourful reflection of a tree in mirror-like water.

the diffusion and absorption are greater. Once the blue has disappeared, then the green disappears too, and the sun turns from yellow-orange to red. The low clouds are then lit with red light and glow red. The sky can acquire a deep-red to purple colour ('heavenly purple') when the atmosphere contains a lot of dust particles, for example after a volcanic eruption. Particularly after sunset it seems as if the sky is on fire. In addition to the colours caused by the particles that are invisible to the naked eye, there are also colours caused by droplets (rainbows) and ice crystals (halos and nacreous clouds), polar lights and 'night clouds'.

Another interesting phenomenon that can sometimes be easy to observe at sunset or sunrise, is the distortion of the sun. The low-lying sun can be reflected in a calm sea surface or against a warm layer of air directly above the sea's surface. In this latter instance the result is a mirage. In both cases a 3-D shape can be discerned.

A green coloration can sometimes be seen at the moment that the sun disappears below the horizon. It is then possible to observe a green beam that lasts for a few seconds and shoots upwards ('green flash').

◁▽High or low? Only the colour (dark/light) of the clouds betrays whether they lie above (lighter) or below (darker) the other clouds.

10 Weather Proverbs

The need to observe weather phenomena and changes in the weather, is forced upon us by our everyday lives, and that has been so since time immemorial. According to Aristotle, it was necessary to study the weather because a practical knowledge of it made life more pleasant and easier. The aim of making observations, was namely to be able to predict the weather, and this was the first step in meteorology. One of the reasons why meteorology as a science was able to develop in Greece, was that there were just enough variations in the type of weather there to make it possible. Too few variations would invite too little interest and too many variations would make it too difficult to be able to say anything about it. Thus Greece is very well situated. The weather is almost entirely determined by the climate; the seasons are well defined: winter and summer weather are called southern and northern weather as a result of the prevailing wind directions. The ancient Greeks, or at least the seafarers, knew not only of four wind

A dark veil of rain often creates a dramatic effect.

directions but also eight others, with specific names that varied in strength and frequency. This considerable number suggests that they made very precise observations.

The first description of a meteorological system is derived from Aristotle (384–322 BC). To be able to understand Aristotle's book *Meteorologica*, the reader has to have some understanding of the state of physics, biology and astronomy that was current then, and we should not forget that the weathervane was the only instrument available to them at that time.
The many books that were written later are often copies of Aristotle's work with a considerable number of additions. In the period 1600–1800, often called the dawn of scientific meteorology, meteorology made great advances as a science through the invention of instruments, such as the thermometer in 1593 (Galileo), the barometer in 1642 (Torricelli) and the hygrometer in 1665 (Robert Hooke). During the many centuries after Aristotle, meteorology was only used because of its practical use, particularly by farmers and seafarers, and it was little more than the popular weather forecast.

Despite the rapid advance in meteorology in the 19th and 20th centuries, weather proverbs have maintained a place of importance. Many general rules and rhymes have arisen throughout the centuries, demonstrating that man

68

The sun just manages to peek through a few holes in this stratocumulus cloud.

has tried to discover some form of system in the weather with the aim of predicting it. The best founded weather proverbs and sayings are those which are connected with the cloud formations, the colour of the sky and the changes in the wind. The large number of sayings in these fields indicate careful observations and the ability to relate phenomena. Let us look at three examples in more detail. The first has to do with the colour of the sky.

Red skies at night,
Shepherd's delight.
Red skies in the morning,
Shepherd's warning.

The sunlight is refracted and diffused in its journey through the atmosphere by the air molecules, water droplets and dust particles. The diffusion is at its greatest for the smallest wave lengths in the spectrum, whilst the diffusing elements also have to be smaller than 1/10 of the wave length of the light. This means that the air molecules diffuse the violet and blue light in particular, giving the sky its blue colour. In the mornings and evenings the sun travels for longer through the atmosphere, so that the longer wave lengths become more diffused, and the water droplets and dust particles are able to make a more important contribution. The green, yellow and red

69

Reflection of sunlight in water. The high light intensity only permits a short shutter time. That is the reason why this backlit photograph looks like it was taken late in the day. The opposite is true.

In this backlit photograph the contrast betwen light and dark is also great. Additional use of a flash prevents objects being photographed as mere silhouettes.

The closer it is to the horizon, the larger the moon appears to be. Looked at absolutely, it is always the same size.

On clear nights the earth's surface cools off considerably. The chance of radiation fog in the morning is then enhanced.

Migrating birds silhouetted before the setting sun.

colours are diffused when the sun is low so that red colours predominate. In the morning there is not much dust in the atmosphere, therefore the cause of red skies at sunrise is water droplets. The red colour indicates that there is much water vapour in the atmosphere and a high chance of rain. This is especially true in the spring and summer. During a period of stable, dry weather, the rising air currents (thermals) carry lots of dust particles into the atmosphere during the day. With the fall in temperature towards the evening, the thermals cease, causing the wind to drop so that the subsequent descending air movements return the dust particles to earth. Red skies at

Below the higher, fine cloud, are dark shreds of clouds (cumulus fractus).

night, seen during dry, stable atmospheric conditions mean that, on the whole, the same kind of weather will be seen the next day. The second example is related to the optical phenomena in the atmosphere.

A ring around the sun or moon,
Means that rain will come real soon.

Or

Ring around the moon,
Rain there will be soon.

74

A light ring at an angle of about 22° around the sun is the most frequently occurring halo phenomenon. Although many people have never noticed a ring around the sun, this occurs on a considerable number of days each year. Usually, a ring is visible in cirrostratus clouds. These clouds are found at an intermediate height of seven kilometres and consist of ice crystals. They look like a fine white veil, sometimes uniformly white and sometimes more or less consisting of threads. The sun and moon shine through them and are still able to cast shadows. The ice crystals are frequently in the form of hexagonal prisms. These hexagonal prisms refract the light in all directions, but at a certain position with respect to the sunlight entering, the refracted light beam has the greatest clarity. Seen from the earth the most suitable angle produces a halo of 22°.

The edge of the extensive bank of stratocumulus is visible on the horizon. The contrasting light/dark effect and their reflection in the water makes the ridge of hills even more conspicuous.

Cirrostratus clouds often occur on the leading edge of a depression, where warm air rises up against cold air. This cloud formation is often the harbinger of thicker clouds that can produce rain: often (about a 70% chance) within the following 24 hours. The approaching depression can, of course, just track past, close by. In the northern hemisphere at our latitudes, the depressions usually track from west to east. Ahead of the depression the wind will often 'back' (turn anti-clockwise) thus announcing the imminent

arrival of a depression, whilst after the depression has passed the wind will 'veer' (turn clockwise) and the rain will be followed by sunshine.

As already stated, the weather proverbs above are based on one or other physical manifestation that is directly related to the weather. Another group of weather sayings is concerned with nature, namely plants and animals. In this case, the assumption is that animals must have certain characteristics to be able to sense approaching danger, so that they can take appropriate steps to avoid it.

When ducks and geese duck and dive,
There'll be rain before five.

If bees stay at home,
Rain will come soon,
If they fly away,
Fine will be the day.

◁*Distortion of the sun caused by differences in the temperatures of various layers of air in the atmosphere.*

The low-lying sun produces a harmony of colour, the drying sandbanks providing regularity in texture.

Sunset, captured by an almost
invisible layer of cloud just above
the horizon.